Eleven Plus
Secondary School Selection

Mathematics

11+
Daily Practice Tests

20 Further Tests
Dual Format

Book 2

© IPS Educational Publishing 2011

Introduction

This second daily maths book is designed to complement the IPS set of 11+ mathematics papers. It contains more short daily practice papers, and uses questions of all of the types covered in the IPS range.

When practising for tests such as the 11+, or other school entrance exams, most people do not use full length practice papers on a daily basis. However, a few minutes of practice every day can be very beneficial, and it does not put too much strain on the pupil who will sit the exam — which is very important indeed.

I would suggest using these papers in between attempting longer practice papers.

Each test should be completed in about six minutes. All the question types used in the IPS range of publications are used in this book. In order to fit the questions on each page we have not left much room for working out. We suggest you use some scrap paper if you need it.

Good luck.

11 Plus team 2011.

© IPS Educational Publishing 2011

Daily Test 1

Question 1

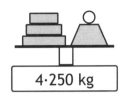

4·250 kg

Sonia places some weights on an electronic scale.
She needs to make a total of 4.90 kg.

Which <u>two</u> of the weights below should she choose to make up the weight to the correct amount?

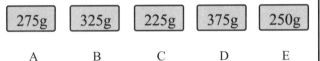

275g	325g	225g	375g	250g
A	B	C	D	E

Circle the <u>two</u> appropriate letters below the weights, or mark the two appropriate letters on the answer sheets.

Question 2

Simone and Becky go to their grandmother's house on the bus each weekday during half term week.
The return journey on the bus costs them £2.40 each.
Each day on the way home they also spend £1.80 for some chips, from the fish and chip shop, which they share.

How much money does mum have to give them to pay for everything during the week?

£ _____

Write your answer in the space provided or mark the appropriate amount on your answer sheet.

Question 3

Northampton   Long Buckley   Rugby   Coventry

A train ran between Northampton and Coventry stations.

There were 60 passengers on the train when it left Northampton.
9 people got out at Long Buckley, and 17 people got on.
Half the passengers left the train at Rugby whilst another 25 got on.

How many people were on the train at Coventry?

_____

Write your answer in the space provided or mark the appropriate number on your answer sheet.

Question 4

Eric spends x pounds each day on bus fares. He spends y pounds each week on train fares.

How much does Eric spend altogether in a fortnight?

A.	$2y + 7x$	☐
B.	$2x + 14y$	☐
C.	$y + 14x$	☐
D.	$7x + 2y$	☐
E.	$14x + 2y$	☐

Place a cross in the box next to the correct equation or mark the appropriate letter on your answer sheet.

Question 5

Look at the shape below.

The shape is made up of 8 identical triangles.
The shaded part has an area of 125cm².

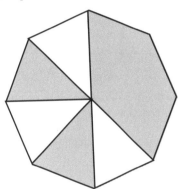

What is the area of the unshaded part?

_____ cm²

Write your answer in the space provided or mark the appropriate number on your answer sheet.

Question 6

Mrs Johnson bought 720 badges to sell in her shop.
They come packed in boxes of 48.

How many boxes of badges did Mrs Johnson buy?

_____ boxes

Write your answer in the space provided or mark the appropriate number on your answer sheet.

© IPS Educational Publishing 2011

Daily Test 2

Question 1

The ratio of flour to sugar in a recipe is 7 : 3.

If 150g of sugar was used for the recipe, how much flour was used?

_____ grams

Write your answer in the space provided or mark the appropriate number on your answer sheet.

Question 2

The spinner shown below has an equal chance of landing on any of the numbers.

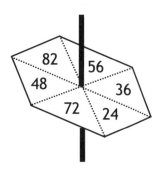

What is the chance that it will come to rest on a number that is a multiple of both 3 and 4?

Write your answer as a fraction in its lowest possible terms.

_____

Write your answer in the space provided or mark the appropriate number on your answer sheet.

Question 3

The hands of the classroom clock show the time 2 o'clock.

What is the acute angle between the hour hand and the minute hand?

_____ °

Write your answer in the space provided or mark the appropriate angle on your answer sheet.

Question 4

During the summer months the local council send a water truck around the area to spray water on the flowerbeds set in the middle of roundabouts. The bar chart below shows how many litres of water were used in a particular week.

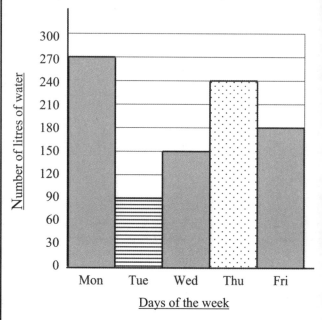

How many more litres were used on Thursday than on Tuesday?

_____

Write your answer in the space provided or mark the appropriate number on your answer sheet.

Question 5

Mr and Mrs Hendry take their 3 children to a football match. Tickets cost £11.00 each for adults. The price of a child's ticket is half that of an adult ticket.

How much does it cost the family to see the match?

£ _____

Write your answer in the space provided or mark the appropriate number on your answer sheet.

Question 6

How many faces would you find on **three** hexahedrons?

_____

Write your answer in the space provided or mark the appropriate number on your answer sheet.

© IPS Educational Publishing 2011

Daily Test 3

Question 1

This is Miya's function machine.

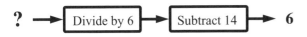

? → | Divide by 6 | → | Subtract 14 | → 6

What number did she start with?

_____

Write your answer in the space provided or mark the appropriate number on your answer sheet.

Question 2

Mr William's class took a survey of the main courses eaten by 120 children in the school canteen one lunchtime.

They counted up the numbers of different meals eaten. This information is shown in the pie chart below.

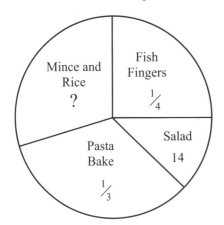

How many children had mince and rice for lunch?

_____

Write your answer in the space provided or mark the appropriate number on your answer sheet.

Question 3

How should a quarter to two in the afternoon be shown on a 24 hour clock?

_____

Write your answer in the space provided or mark the appropriate time on your answer sheet.

Question 4

Look at the net below. When folded it makes a box.

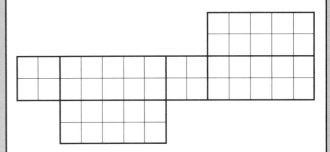

If the side of each small square is 5 cm, what will be the total volume of the box?

_____ cm³

Write your answer in the space provided or mark the appropriate number on your answer sheet.

Question 5

There are 32 children in Mr Simmonds' class. 12 girls and 20 boys.
One child's name is chosen at random to collect in the homework on Monday morning.

What is the chance that the child will be a girl?

(Show your answer as a fraction in its lowest terms.)

_____

Write your answer in the space provided or mark the appropriate number on your answer sheet.

Question 6

150 children took part in a "Guess the age of the head teacher" competition to raise money for charity.

? guessed too high. 84 guessed too low.

How many children guessed the head teacher's correct age?

_____

Write your answer in the space provided or mark the appropriate number on your answer sheet.

© IPS Educational Publishing 2011

Question 1

Laura has seven 50 pence pieces, one 20 pence piece, two 10 pence pieces and five 5 pence pieces in her purse.

How much money does she have in total?

£ _____

Write your answer in the space provided or mark the appropriate number on your answer sheet.

Question 2

This is a map of the classrooms in St George's school. You must try to find your way from <u>Mrs Smith's class</u> to <u>Mr Monkton's class</u> using a set of instructions.

Key to the instructions:
FD means forward, **RT** means turn right 90° and **LT** means turn left 90°.

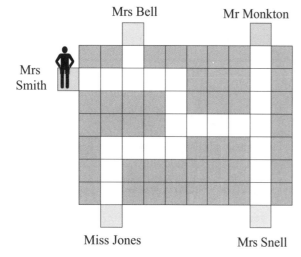

Which of these sets of instructions is the correct one? Circle the appropriate letter or mark the appropriate letter on your answer sheet.

A. FD 5, RT, FD 2, LT, FD 4, LT, FD 4.

B. FD 6, RT, FD 3, LT, FD 4, RT, FD 3.

C. FD 5, LT, FD 2, RT, FD 4, RT, FD 4.

D. FD 6, RT, FD 2, LT, FD 4, RT, FD 3.

E. FD 5, RT, FD 3, RT, FD 4, LT, FD 4.

Question 3

Jane's mother is twice as old as Jane will be in 9 years time.

If Jane is 8, then how old is her mother? _____

Write your answer in the space provided or mark the appropriate number on your answer sheet.

Question 4

Ahmed had the job of totalling the money made on five stalls at the summer fair. In the five tins he found £7.20 £8.40, £7.60, £11.50 and £5.30.

How much did the five stalls make in total?

£ _____

Write your answer in the space provided or mark the appropriate amount on your answer sheet.

Question 5

This graph shows the conversion rate between Japanese Yen (¥) and UK Pounds (£).

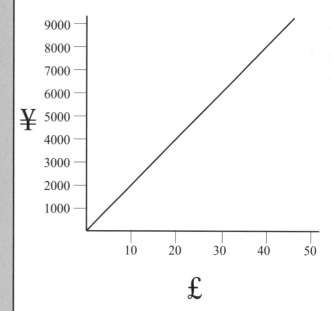

How many pounds (£) would I need to change to get ¥8000?

£ _____

Write your answer in the space provided or mark the appropriate number on your answer sheet.

Question 6

Smithton Primary school went on a school trip to the sea. The coach set off at 8.30 and drove for 1 hour 50 minutes before stopping for 20 minutes for a comfort break. After another 1 hour and a half they arrived at the seaside.

At what time did they arrive? _____

Write your answer in the space provided or mark the appropriate time on your answer sheet.

© IPS Educational Publishing 2011

Daily Test 5

Question 1

Which of these sets of numbers contains all square numbers?

A.	81	63	36	☐
B.	63	25	16	☐
C.	121	64	49	☐
D.	90	81	49	☐
E.	144	99	810	☐

Place a cross in the box or mark the appropriate letter on your answer sheet.

Question 2

Look at the Venn diagram below. It shows how many children in Mrs Chandler's class like baked beans, peas or both. 3 children like neither. There are 28 children in the class. Some numbers are missing from the diagram.

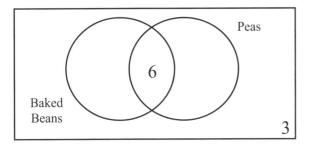

If 19 children like baked beans:

How many children in the class like peas?

(_____)

Write your answer in the space provided or mark the appropriate number on your answer sheet.

Question 3

In this question you must find the missing number so that the equation balances.

$$9 \times 5 + 19 = 24 \div 3 \times \underline{\hspace{2cm}}$$

Write your answer in the space provided or mark the appropriate number on your answer sheet.

Question 4

24	37	50
50	63	76
63	76	

There is a number missing on this grid.

What is it?   (_____)

Write your answer in the space provided or mark the appropriate number on your answer sheet.

Question 4

Look at the diagram below:

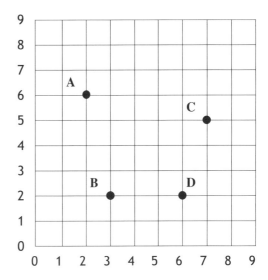

What are the co-ordinates of the points at letter A and letter D?

A ____ , ____

D ____ , ____

Write the co-ordinates in the spaces provided or mark the appropriate pair on your answer sheet.

Question 6

There are 15 fish fingers in a jumbo packet.

How many packets would you fill with 645 fish fingers?

_____ packets

Write your answer in the space provided or mark the appropriate number on your answer sheet.

© IPS Educational Publishing 2011

Daily Test 6

Question 1

Three corners of a square have the co-ordinates (12, 3) (6, 9) and (6, 3).

What are the co-ordinates of the fourth corner?

(_____ , _____)

Write your answer in the space provided or mark the appropriate co-ordinates on your answer sheet.

Question 2

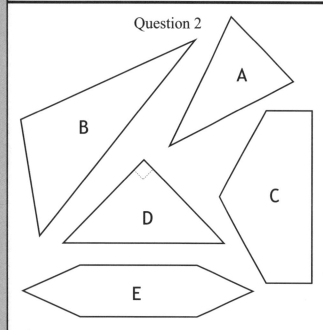

Which one of the shapes above has twice as many acute angles than obtuse angles?

Circle the letter in one of the shapes or mark the appropriate letter on your answer sheet.

Question 3

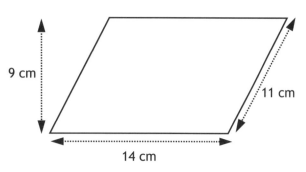

9 cm

11 cm

14 cm

What is the total area of the parallelogram?

_____ cm^2

Write your answer in the space provided or mark the appropriate number on your answer sheet.

Question 4

Look at the graph to the left.

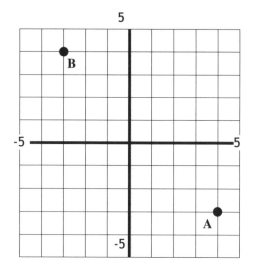

What are the co-ordinates of A and B?

	A	B	
A.	(-4, 3)	(3, -4)	☐
B.	(4, -3)	(-3, 4)	☐
C.	(-3, 4)	(3, -4)	☐
D.	(4, -3)	(-4, 3)	☐
E.	(-3, 4)	(4, -3)	☐

Place a cross in the correct box or mark the appropriate letter on your answer sheet.

Question 5

Look at the following number.

90.984949

What is this number to 3 (three) decimal places?

_____

Write you answer in the space provided or mark the appropriate number on your answer sheet.

Question 6

Complete the following sequence:

3,   7,   15,   31,   63,   _____

Write your answer in the space provided or mark the appropriate number on your answer sheet.

© IPS Educational Publishing 2011

Question 1

This is a magic square.

	Z	15
17		13

All the columns, rows and diagonals add up to 48.

Several numbers have been missed out.

What number should replace the letter **Z** ?

_____

Write your answer in the space provided or mark the appropriate number on your answer sheet.

Question 2

Roger places 12 balls into a black bag. Five are yellow, three are green and four are blue.
He takes **two** balls at random from the bag and places them on the table. Both balls are yellow.

What is the chance that the next ball out of the bag will be another yellow one?

$\frac{1}{5}$	$\frac{5}{12}$	$\frac{3}{10}$	$\frac{2}{5}$	$\frac{1}{4}$
A	B	C	D	E

Circle the appropriate letter or mark the appropriate letter on your answer sheet.

Question 3

Johnnie and Yvonne take the bus home from school every weekday during the winter.

Yvonne pays 55p a day to ride on the bus. Johnnie pays an extra 30p a day because he travels 5 stops further than Yvonne.

How much does it cost them altogether to go home on the bus for **two** weeks?

£ _____

Write your answer in the space provided or mark the appropriate amount on your answer sheet.

Question 4

Look at the nets below.

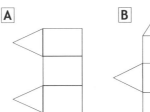

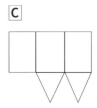
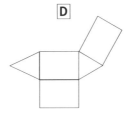
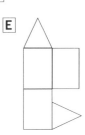

Which one of these nets is the only one that will fold to form a **triangular** prism?

Circle the letter next to the correct net or mark the appropriate letter on your answer sheet.

Question 5

Look at the numbers below.

50.019	49.909	49.982	50.101	49.899
A	B	C	D	E

Which of the following numbers has a value closest to 50?

Circle the appropriate letter or mark the appropriate letter on your answer sheet.

Question 6

Mrs Thomas buys nine, 5 litre bottles of spring water from the supermarket.

Approximately how much do they weigh altogether?

Your answer should be in kilograms.

_____Kg

Write your answer in the space provided or mark the appropriate weight on your answer sheet.

© IPS Educational Publishing 2011

Question 1

Lisa, Sally, Kathryn, Gillian and Emma each bought a new top from the shop StyleGirl.

Sally paid £12.50, Emma £11.99, Kathryn £14.10, Gillian £8.49 and Lisa £13.75.

What was the range of the prices paid?

£_____

Write your answer in the space provided or mark the appropriate box on your answer sheet.

Question 2

Which of these shapes have 4 lines of symmetry? (There could be more than one)

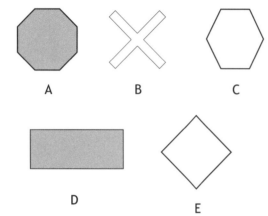

Circle the correct letter/s or mark the appropriate letters on your answer sheet.

Question 3

Bert's aunt takes Bert and his three friends, Bill, Bob and Ben, on a steam railway trip to the Scotland and back.

It costs £68.00 for adults. Children's tickets are half price.

Luckily, Bert's aunt has a voucher which gives them an extra 50% off the cost of the trip.

How much did the trip cost Bert's aunt altogether?

£_____

Write your answer in the space provided or mark the appropriate amount on your answer sheet.

Question 4

Mr Jupitus, the head teacher, went to the local shop to buy some sausages for the school summer barbeque.
In the shop there were 5 different packs at 5 different prices:

A.	Big Bangers	£6.00 / pack of 20
B.	Vernon's Veggies	£2.40 / pack of 6
C.	Lincolnshire Sausages	£3.65 / pack of 10
D.	Sausage Supreme	£10.00 / pack of 25
E.	Organic Specials	£8.00 / pack of 16

Which pack contains sausages at the lowest price each?

A   B   C   D   E

Circle the correct letter or mark the appropriate letter on your answer sheet.

Question 5

Kurt, Billy, Shannon and Eloise all collected money for charity by taking part in a sponsored silence.

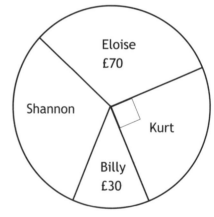

Between them they collected £240. They drew a pie chart to show how much each of them had collected.

How much did Shannon collect?   £ _____

Write your answer in the space provided or mark the appropriate number on your answer sheet.

Question 6

If $7g - 19 = 79$, then what is the value of g ?

$$g = \_\_\_\_$$

Write your answer in the space provided or mark the appropriate number on your answer sheet.

© IPS Educational Publishing 2011

Daily Test 9

Question 1

The local stationery shop has a sale.
Every item in the shop is reduced by 30%.
Mrs Cartwright buys a big box of paper for her printer.
It normally costs £16.50.

How much does Mrs Cartwright have to pay for the paper in the sale?

£ _____

Write your answer in the space provided or mark the appropriate number on your answer sheet.

Question 2

Look carefully at the grid below.

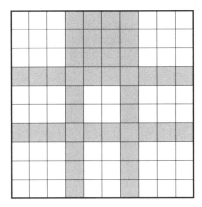

What percentage of this grid has been shaded?

_____%

Write your answer in the space provided or mark the appropriate percentage on your answer sheet.

Question 3

Which of the figures below shows the number

Six hundred and sixteen thousand and sixteen.

A.   661616   ☐
B.   600616   ☐
C.   616160   ☐
D.   601616   ☐
E.   616016   ☐

Place a cross in the box next to the correct number or mark the appropriate letter on your answer sheet.

Question 4

This half term Angelo has taken 10 tables tests.
Here are his results out of 20:

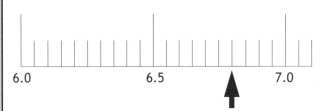

16   13   11   13   19   14   15   9   18   12

What was his <u>mean</u> score?

_____

Write your answer in the space provided or mark the appropriate number on your answer sheet.

Question 5

Look at the number line below.

6.0   6.5   7.0

What is the value of the number that the arrow is pointing towards?

_____

Write your answer in the space provided or mark the appropriate number on your answer sheet.

Question 6

Mrs Campbell's class did a survey in their school on their top five favourite pets. They then produced this chart.

Favourite Pets	
Key: ☐ stands for 5 children ■ stands for 1 child	
Dogs	☐☐☐☐■■■
Hamsters/Mice	☐☐■
Fish	☐■■■■
Cats	☐☐☐☐☐■■
Rabbits	☐☐☐☐■■■■

How many children listed Rabbits as their favourite pet?

_____

Write your answer in the space provided or mark the appropriate time on your answer sheet.

© IPS Educational Publishing 2011

Daily Test 10

Score. _____

Question 1

What fraction of a day is 15 hours?

Write your answer in its lowest possible terms.

_____

Write your answer in the space provided or mark the appropriate fraction on your answer sheet.

Question 2

The product of 2 numbers is 60.

The difference between the two numbers is 11.

What are the two numbers?

_____   _____

Write your answers in the spaces provided or mark the appropriate numbers on your answer sheet.

Question 3

Look carefully at the graph below.

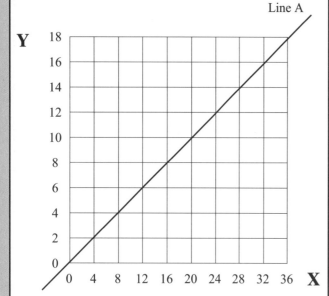

What is the rule that governs the plotting of line A?

Circle the appropriate letter.

A. $2Y + 2 = X$

B. $X = Y + 1$

C. $2X = Y \div 2$

D. $X \div 2 = Y$

E. $2Y = X + 2$

Write your answer in the space provided or mark the appropriate number on your answer sheet.

Question 4

In a shop there are 850 DVDs.
275 are sold to customers over the counter.
123 are sold on the internet.

How many DVDs remain unsold?

_____ DVDs

Write your answer in the space provided or mark the appropriate number on your answer sheet.

Question 5

This is a floor plan of the local supermarket.

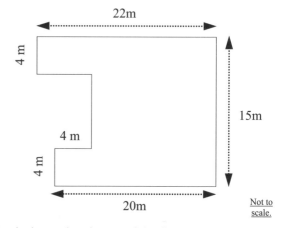

Not to scale.

What is the total perimeter of the floor?

_____ m

Write your answer in the space provided or mark the appropriate number on your answer sheet.

Question 6

Augusta is flying to Vancouver in Canada for a holiday with her family.
There is a time difference between Great Britain and Vancouver.
Vancouver is 8 hours behind Augusta's home in London .

It takes 9½ hours to fly from London to Vancouver.

If Augusta's plane leaves London at midday what will the time be in Vancouver when her plane lands?

(Remember to state AM or PM)

_____

Write your answer in the space provided or mark the appropriate time on your answer sheet.

© IPS Educational Publishing 2011

Daily Test 11

Question 1

101	86	71
86	71	56
71	56	

There is a number missing on this grid.

What is it? _____

Write your answer in the space provided or mark the appropriate number on your answer sheet.

Question 2

Look at the diagram below:

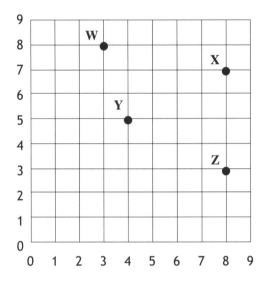

What are the co-ordinates of the points at letter Y and letter X?

Y ____ , ____

X ____ , ____

Write the co-ordinates in the spaces provided or mark the appropriate pair your answer sheet.

Question 3

Jenna's cousin is 3 times as old as Jenna was 5 years ago.

If Jenna's cousin is 24, how old is Jenna? _____

Write your answer in the space provided or mark the appropriate number on your answer sheet.

Question 4

Which of these sets of numbers contains <u>no</u> square numbers?

A.	46	49	72	☐
B.	16	36	56	☐
C.	36	49	144	☐
D.	72	120	121	☐
E.	21	45	90	☐

Place a cross in the box or mark the appropriate letter on your answer sheet.

Question 5

Look at the Venn diagram below. It shows how many children in Mr Bunting's class play chess, draughts or both. 5 children play neither. There are 33 children in the class.

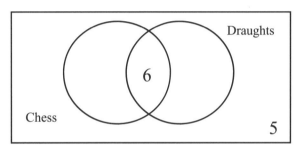

If 25 children play chess:

How many children in the class play draughts in total?

_____

Write your answer in the space provided or mark the appropriate number on your answer sheet.

Question 6

In this question you must find the missing number so that the equation balances.

$$66 \div 11 \times 8 = 120 \div 5 + \underline{\quad}$$

Write your answer in the space provided or mark the appropriate number on your answer sheet.

© IPS Educational Publishing 2011

Daily Test 12

Question 1

Mrs Jennings has been collecting for charity.
She has collected lots of money in her tin. In the last four days she has collected £12.25, £13.55, £9.65 and £11.48.

How much has she collected in total?

£ _____

Write your answer in the space provided or mark the appropriate amount on your answer sheet.

Question 2

In the diagram below, 1 small square represents 1cm²

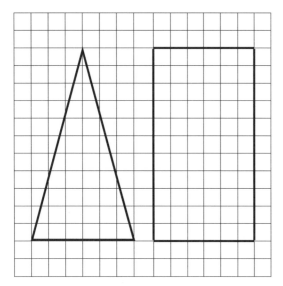

What is the difference between the area of the rectangle and the area of the triangle?

18cm²   33cm²   26cm²   22cm²   36cm²

A   B   C   D   E

Circle the appropriate letter or mark the appropriate letter on your answer sheet.

Question 3

Miranda has drawn a plan of a football pitch. She has used a scale of 1cm to 6m.

On her plan the side of the pitch measures 12cm.

What is the actual length of the football pitch?

_____metres

Write your answer in the space provided or mark the appropriate box on your answer sheet.

Question 4

Sam has eight 50 pence pieces, six 20 pence pieces, one 10 pence piece and three 5 pence pieces in her pocket.

How much money does she have in total?

£ _____

Write your answer in the space provided or mark the appropriate amount on your answer sheet.

Question 5

This is a map of part of St John's school. You must try to find your way from the Head's Office to the Library using a set of instructions.

Key to the instructions:
FD means forward, **RT** means turn right 90º and **LT** means turn left 90º.

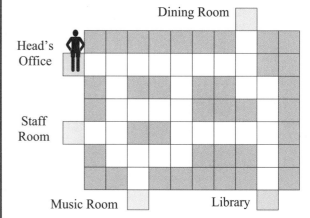

Which of these sets of instructions is the correct one?

A.   FD 5, RT, FD 3, RT, FD 4, RT, FD 3.

B.   FD 8 , LT, FD 5, LT, FD 2, RT, FD 6.

C.   FD 2, LT, FD 3, RT, FD 5, RT, FD 3.

D.   FD 5, RT, FD 3, LT, FD 4, RT, FD 3.

E.   FD 2, RT, FD 3, LT, FD 8, RT, FD 6.

Circle the appropriate letter or mark the appropriate letter on your answer sheet.

Question 6

There are 25 erasers in a box.

How many boxes could you fill with 425 erasers?

_____ boxes

Write your answer in the space provided or mark the appropriate number on your answer sheet.

© IPS Educational Publishing 2011

Daily Test 13

Question 1

Look at the net below. When folded it makes a box.

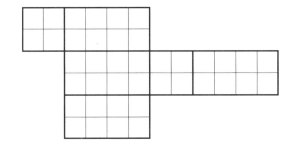

If the side of each small square is 5 cm, what will be the total surface area of the box?

_____ cm²

Write your answer in the space provided or mark the appropriate number on your answer sheet.

Question 2

There are 50 children on a bus, 35 girls and 15 boys. One child's name is chosen at random to collect the tickets.

What is the chance that the child will be a girl?

(Show your answer as a fraction in its lowest terms.)

_____

Write your answer in the space provided or mark the appropriate fraction on your answer sheet.

Question 3

If the perimeter of a rectangle is 18cm, which of the following *could* be the area of that rectangle?

    A. 18cm²

    B. 10cm²

    C. 24cm²

    D. 36cm²

    E. 30cm²

Circle the correct letter or mark the appropriate box on your answer sheet.

Question 4

This is Geoff's function machine.

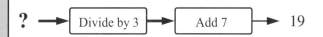

What number did he start with?

_____

Write your answer in the space provided or mark the appropriate number on your answer sheet.

Question 5

Roger, Simon, Kamran, James and Rahul all stood for election to become captain of the cricket club.

240 people voted for which person they wanted to be captain. The results showing the number of votes cast are shown in pie chart below. Unfortunately they have mixed fractions, percentages and numbers.

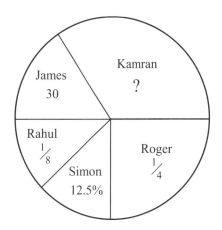

How many votes did Kamran receive? _____

Write your answer in the space provided or mark the appropriate number on your answer sheet.

Question 6

How should a quarter to seven in the evening appear on a 24 hour clock?

_____

Write your answer in the space provided or mark the appropriate time on your answer sheet.

© IPS Educational Publishing 2011

Daily Test 14

Question 1

The ratio of boys to girls in a music class is 4 : 5.

If there are 36 children in the class, how many of them are boys?

_____

Write your answer in the space provided or mark the appropriate number on your answer sheet.

Question 2

The spinner shown below has an equal chance of landing on any of the numbers.

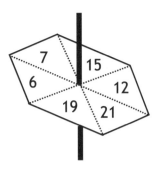

What is the chance that it will come to rest on a number that is a prime number?

Write your answer as a fraction in its lowest possible terms.

_____

Write your answer in the space provided or mark the appropriate fraction on your answer sheet.

Question 3

The hands of the classroom clock show the time 9 o'clock.

What is the size of the reflex angle between the hour hand and the minute hand?

_____ °

Write your answer in the space provided or mark the appropriate angle on your answer sheet.

Question 4

Five children collected aluminium cans for the school recycling drive. The bar chart below shows how many cans each of the children collected.

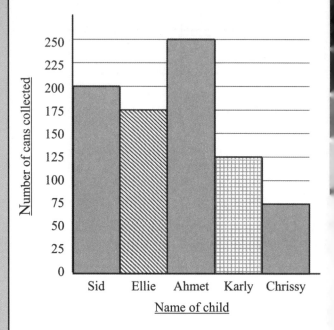

How many more cans were collected by Ahmet than by Chrissy?

_____

Write your answer in the space provided or mark the appropriate number on your answer sheet.

Question 5

Miss Jennings takes 5 pupils to see a free exhibition in London. Train tickets cost £6.80 each for child. The price of a adult's ticket is £3.20 more than that of a child.

How much does it cost in total to visit the exhibition?

£ _____

Write your answer in the space provided or mark the appropriate number on your answer sheet.

Question 6

How many faces would you find on a shape made by two identical cubes that have been stuck together face to face?

_____

Write your answer in the space provided or mark the appropriate number on your answer sheet.

© IPS Educational Publishing 2011

Daily Test 15

Question 1

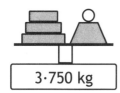

3·750 kg

Jenny places some weights on an electronic scale.
She needs to make a total of 4.250 kg.

Which two of the weights below should she choose to make up the weight to the correct amount?

375g	175g	225g	125g	350g
A	B	C	D	E

Circle the two appropriate letters below the weights, or mark the two appropriate letters on the answer sheets.

Question 2

Chris and Vinny go to an after school club each weekday during the Spring term.
They have to pay 75p a day each to attend.
They also pay an extra 35p a day to have a drink.

How much will it cost the pair of them to go to the after school club for one week?

£ _____

Write your answer in the space provided or mark the appropriate amount on your answer sheet.

Question 3

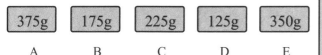

Thorpe Culvert   Wainfleet   Havenhouse   Skegness

A train ran between Thorpe Culvert and Skegness railway stations.

There were 57 passengers on the train when it left Thorpe Culvert.
8 people got out at Wainfleet, and 19 people got on.
23 left the train at Havenhouse whilst 29 got on.

How many people were on the train at when it arrived at Skegness?

_____

Write your answer in the space provided or mark the appropriate number on your answer sheet.

Question 4

Mum gives y pounds pocket money to John each week and x pounds pocket money to Jenny each month.

How much does mum give them in total in a year?

A. $7y + 12x$ ☐

B. $52x + 12y$ ☐

C. $12y + 7x$ ☐

D. $12x + 52y$ ☐

E. $10x + 12y$ ☐

Place a cross in the box next to the correct expression or mark the appropriate letter on your answer sheet.

Question 5

Look at the shape below.

The area of the shape that is coloured black is 27 cm².

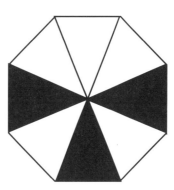

What area of the shape is unshaded?

_____ cm²

Write your answer in the space provided or mark the appropriate number on your answer sheet.

Question 6

Mr Frederick bought 13500 printed shopping bags for his customers at the local supermarket.
They come packed in boxes of 45.

How many boxes of shopping bags did Mr Frederick buy?

_____ boxes

Write your answer in the space provided or mark the appropriate number on your answer sheet.

© IPS Educational Publishing 2011

Daily Test 16

Question 1

Jack Joiner, the carpenter, bought a box of 1,000 screws.
He used 239 screws on one job.
366 were used on his next job.

How many screws remain unused?

_____

Write your answer in the space provided or mark the appropriate number on your answer sheet.

Question 2

This is a plan of the patio Mrs Jenkins wants to build.

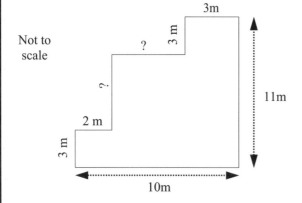

How many 1m² paving slabs does she need to cover the patio?

_____ slabs

Write your answer in the space provided or mark the appropriate number on your answer sheet.

Question 3

Yasmeen is flying to Karachi in Pakistan to visit her grandparents.
There is a time difference between Great Britain and Karachi. Yasmeen's home in Birmingham is 5 hours behind her grandparents home in Karachi.

It takes 8 hours to fly from Birmingham to Karachi.

If Yasmeen's plane leaves Birmingham at 8am what will the time be in Karachi when her plane touches down?

(Remember to state AM or PM)

_____

Write your answer in the space provided or mark the appropriate time on your answer sheet.

Question 4

What fraction of a day is 4 hours?

Write your answer in its lowest possible terms.

_____

Write your answer in the space provided or mark the appropriate fraction on your answer sheet.

Question 5

The product of 2 numbers is 48.
The difference between the two numbers is 13.

What are the two numbers?

_____   _____

Write your answers in the space provided or mark the two appropriate numbers on your answer sheet.

Question 6

Look carefully at the graph below.

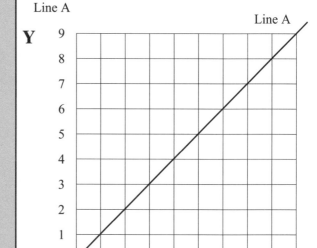

What is the rule that governs the plotting of line A?

Circle the appropriate letter.

A.   X + 1 = Y

B.   Y - 2 = X

C.   X = 2Y

D.   Y = X - 2

E.   2Y - X = Y

Write your answer in the space provided or mark the appropriate letter on your answer sheet.

© IPS Educational Publishing 2011

Daily Test 17

Question 1

This half term Nicola has taken 9 spelling tests. Here are her results out of 20:

14   11   14   11   8   16   15   18   10

What was her <u>mean</u> score?

_____

Write your answer in the space provided or mark the appropriate number on your answer sheet.

Question 2

Look at the number line below.

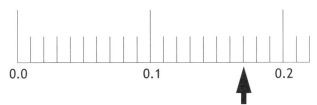

0.0   0.1   0.2

What is the value of the number that the arrow is pointing towards?

_____

Write your answer in the space provided or mark the appropriate number on your answer sheet.

Question 3

Mrs Campbell's class did a survey in their school on favourite types of music.

Favourite Types of Music	
Key: □ stands for 4 children ■ stands for 1 children	
Heavy Metal	□□■
Brass Band	□■■
Hip Hop	□□■■■
Classical	■■■
Pop	□□□□■■

How many more children liked Pop than Hip Hop?

_____

Write your answer in the space provided or mark the appropriate number on your answer sheet.

Question 4

The local mobile phone shop has a sale.
Every item in the shop is reduced by 25%.
Georgie buys a new telephone.
It normally costs £90.00.

How much does Georgie have to pay for the phone in the sale?

£ _____

Write your answer in the space provided or mark the appropriate amount on your answer sheet.

Question 5

Look carefully at the grid below.

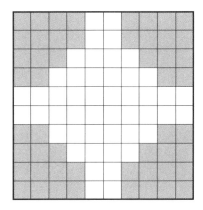

What percentage of this grid is coloured white?

_____%

Write your answer in the space provided or mark the appropriate percentage on your answer sheet.

Question 6

Which of the figures below shows the number

Seventy-seven thousand and seventy-seven.

A.	770077	□
B.	77770	□
C.	77077	□
D.	707077	□
E.	7777	□

Place a cross in the box next to the correct number or mark the appropriate letter on your answer sheet.

© IPS Educational Publishing 2011

Daily Test 18

Question 1

Below are some prices from the local bakery.

Vanilla Slice	80p each
Raspberry Jam Doughnut	50p each
Chocolate Éclair	90p each
Fairy Cake	30p each
Individual Bakewell Tart	45p each

How much would it cost to buy 4 fairy cakes, 2 chocolate éclairs and one each of the remaining 3 types of cake?

£3.75	£4.75	£4.10	£4.45	£5.05
A	B	C	D	E

Circle the correct letter or mark in the appropriate box on your answer sheet.

Question 2

The children in all the local schools took part in a vote to find out which was their favourite pop group. The results are shown in this pie chart.

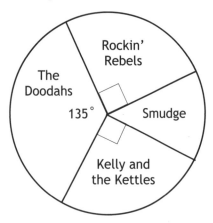

In all 2000 children took part in the vote.

How many votes did "Smudge" receive? _____

Write your answer in the space provided or mark the appropriate number on your answer sheet.

Question 3

If $6t - 12 = 60$, then what is the value of t ?

$$t = \_\_\_\_$$

Write your answer in the space provided or mark the appropriate number on your answer sheet.

Question 4

Juanita, Shahnaz, Laura, Sally and Joanie each bought a CD from the local supermarket.

Joanie paid £8.49, Shahnaz £9.99, Laura £5.69, Juanita £10.99 and Sally £7.89.

What was the range of the prices paid?

£_____

Write your answer in the space provided or mark the appropriate box on your answer sheet.

Question 5

Which of these shapes has a rotational symmetry of order 2?

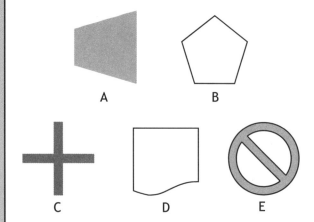

Circle the correct letter/s or mark the appropriate letter/s on your answer sheet.

Question 6

Mervyn's grandma takes Mervyn and his three friends to Frumton zoo for a treat.

It costs £8.00 for adults and £4.00 each for children. Each child also bought an ice cream and Mervyn's grandma had a cup of coffee.

Ice creams are £1.50 each and cups of coffee cost £1.20.

How much did the trip cost Mervyn's grandma altogether?

£_____

Write your answer in the space provided or mark the appropriate amount on your answer sheet.

© IPS Educational Publishing 2011

Question 1

This is a magic square.

18		12
14	X	

All the columns, rows and diagonals add up to 39.

Several numbers have been missed out.

What number should replace the letter *X* ?

_____

Write your answer in the space provided or mark the appropriate number on your answer sheet.

Question 2

Rebecca places 13 balls into a black bag. Five are green, four are red and four are blue.

She takes one ball at random from the bag and places it on the table. It is red.

What is the chance that the next ball out of the bag will be blue?

$\frac{1}{4}$ $\frac{4}{13}$ $\frac{4}{9}$ $\frac{5}{12}$ $\frac{1}{3}$

A   B   C   D   E

Circle the appropriate letter or mark the appropriate letter on your answer sheet.

Question 3

Sam's mum buys eight, 2 litre bottles of lemonade and six litre bottles of cola from the supermarket.
Approximately how much do the eight bottles weigh altogether?

Your answer should be in kilograms.

_____Kg

Write your answer in the space provided or mark the appropriate weight on your answer sheet.

Question 4

Look at the nets below.

A   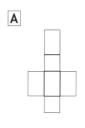   B   C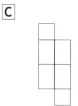

D   E

Which of these nets will fold to form a **cuboid?**
There could be more than one.

Circle the letter/s next to the correct net/s or mark the appropriate letters on your answer sheet.

Question 5

Three brothers, Basil, Charlie and Nikolas, go to a football training camp each weekday morning during the holidays. They each have to pay £1.10 a day to attend. They have to pay extra for drinks. Charlie buys one each day, whilst the others have two. The drinks cost 50p.

How much will it cost altogether for the three of them to attend football training for one week?

£ _____

Write your answer in the space provided or mark the appropriate amount on your answer sheet.

Question 6

Look at the numbers below.

Which of the following numbers has a value closest to 15?

14.909   15.101   14.190   14.995   14.899

A   B   C   D   E

Circle the appropriate letter or mark the appropriate number on your answer sheet.

© IPS Educational Publishing 2011

Daily Test 20

Score. _____

Question 1

Three corners of a rectangle have the co-ordinates (4, 9) (9,9) and (4,2).

What are the co-ordinates of the fourth corner?

(_____ , _____)

Write your answer in the space provided or mark the appropriate co-ordinates on your answer sheet.

Question 2

Look at the shapes below.

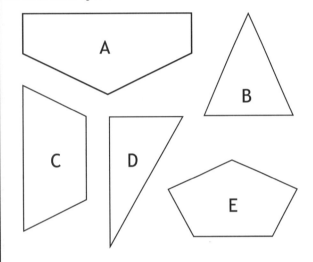

Which of these shapes contains two obtuse angles?

Circle the letter in one of the shapes or mark the appropriate letter on your answer sheet.

Question 3

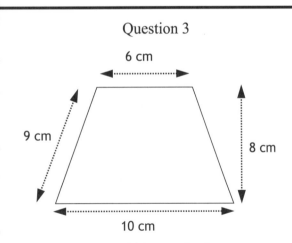

6 cm

9 cm

8 cm

10 cm

What is the total area of this trapezium?

_____ cm²

Write your answer in the space provided or mark the appropriate number on your answer sheet.

Question 4

Look at the graph below.

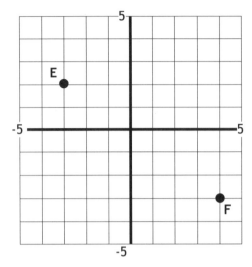

What are the co-ordinates of E and F?

	E	F
A.	(2, -3)	(3, -4)	☐
B.	(-3, -2)	(3, -4)	☐
C.	(3, -2)	(-4, 3)	☐
D.	(-3, 2)	(4, -3)	☐
E.	(-2, 3)	(4, 3)	☐

Place a cross in the correct box or mark the appropriate letter on your answer sheet.

Question 5

Look at the following number.

19.94865

What is this number to 2 (two) decimal places?

_____

Write your answer in the space provided or mark the appropriate number on your answer sheet.

Question 6

Complete the following sequence:

12,   9,   18,   15,   30,   27,   _____

Write your answer in the space provided or mark the appropriate number on your answer sheet.

© IPS Educational Publishing 2011

Multiple choice answer sheet.   Tests 1 to 6.

1

1: A B C D E

2: £37.00, £33.00, £42.00, £21.00, £25.80

3: 54, 52, 51, 59, 57

4: A B C D E

5: 75 cm², 105 cm², 95 cm², 80 cm², 100 cm²

6: 18, 20, 15, 22, 12

2

1: 500 grams, 350 grams, 400 grams, 450 grams, 300 grams

2: 2/6, 5/6, 1/3   2/3, 1/2

3: 40°, 230°, 60°, 80°, 300°

4: 100, 110, 120, 150, 90

5: £33.00, £38.50, £44.00, £27.50, £40.50

6: 15, 24, 27, 18, 21

3

1: 48, 72, 120, 80, 150

2: 36, 54, 40, 45, 30

3: 0215, 01.45, 13.45, 1.45, 1345

4: 2500 cm², 1250 cm², 250 cm², 500 cm², 125 cm²

5: 2/3, 5/8, 1/2   2/6, 3/8

6: 16, 20, 18, 25, 10

4

1: £3.65, £4.15, £3.95, £3.85, £3.75

2: A B C D E

3: 34, 38, 40, 36, 32

4: £37.90, £38.50, £41.20, £40.00, £36.50

5: £35, £30, £45, £50, £40

6: 12.30, 11.50, 13.30, 12.10, 11.30

5

1: A B C D E

2: 15, 9, 10, 12, 6

3: 8, 6, 4, 9, 12

4: 99, 79, 86, 89, 96

5: A 6,2 D 2,6 / A 6,2 D 6,2 / A 7,3 D 2,6 / A 2,6 D 6,2 / A 3,7 D 6,2

6: 50, 43, 39, 45, 48

6

1: 9,12, 3,12, 12,9, 6,12, 3,6

2: A B C D E

3: 126 cm², 154 cm², 140 cm², 99 cm², 160 cm²

4: A B C D E

5: 90.984, 90.980, 91.000, 90.985, 90.990

6: 91, 118, 99, 94, 127

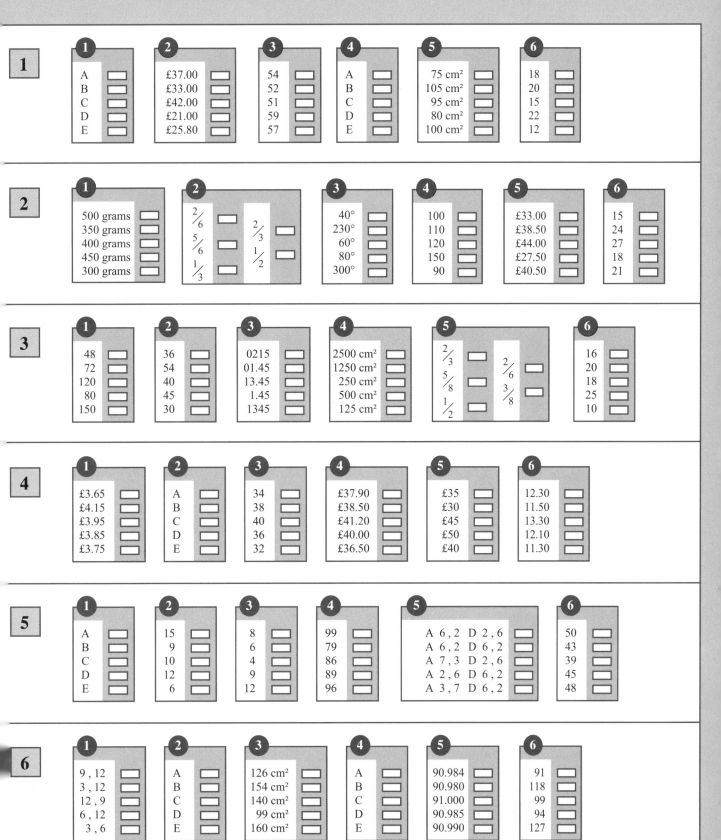

© IPS Educational Publishing 2011

Multiple choice answer sheet.   Tests 7 to 12.

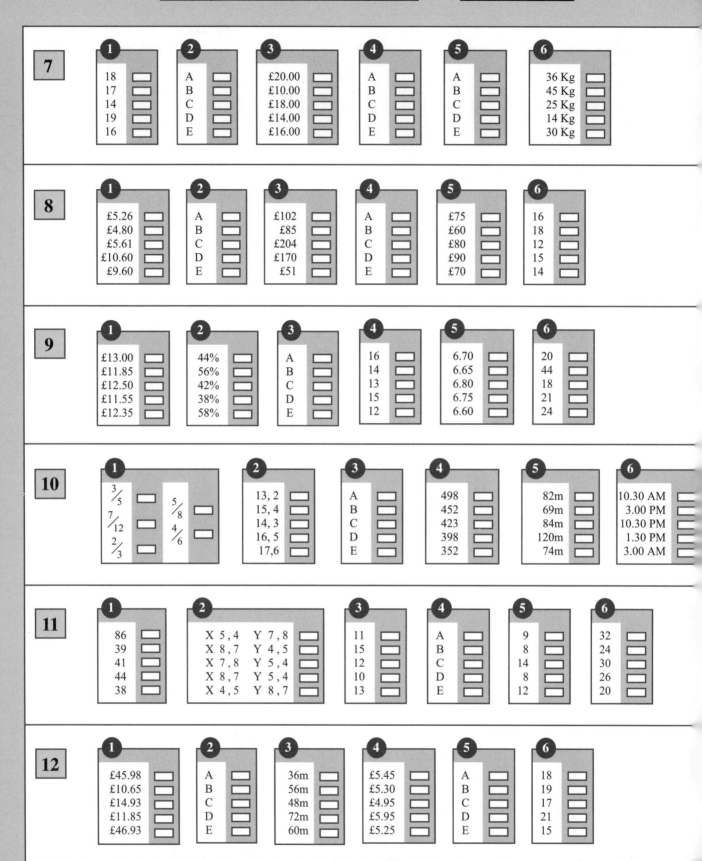

7

1: 18, 17, 14, 19, 16
2: A, B, C, D, E
3: £20.00, £10.00, £18.00, £14.00, £16.00
4: A, B, C, D, E
5: A, B, C, D, E
6: 36 Kg, 45 Kg, 25 Kg, 14 Kg, 30 Kg

8

1: £5.26, £4.80, £5.61, £10.60, £9.60
2: A, B, C, D, E
3: £102, £85, £204, £170, £51
4: A, B, C, D, E
5: £75, £60, £80, £90, £70
6: 16, 18, 12, 15, 14

9

1: £13.00, £11.85, £12.50, £11.55, £12.35
2: 44%, 56%, 42%, 38%, 58%
3: A, B, C, D, E
4: 16, 14, 13, 15, 12
5: 6.70, 6.65, 6.80, 6.75, 6.60
6: 20, 44, 18, 21, 24

10

1: $\frac{3}{5}$, $\frac{7}{12}$, $\frac{2}{3}$, $\frac{5}{8}$, $\frac{4}{6}$
2: 13, 2; 15, 4; 14, 3; 16, 5; 17,6
3: A, B, C, D, E
4: 498, 452, 423, 398, 352
5: 82m, 69m, 84m, 120m, 74m
6: 10.30 AM, 3.00 PM, 10.30 PM, 1.30 PM, 3.00 AM

11

1: 86, 39, 41, 44, 38
2: X 5,4 Y 7,8; X 8,7 Y 4,5; X 7,8 Y 5,4; X 8,7 Y 5,4; X 4,5 Y 8,7
3: 11, 15, 12, 10, 13
4: A, B, C, D, E
5: 9, 8, 14, 8, 12
6: 32, 24, 30, 26, 20

12

1: £45.98, £10.65, £14.93, £11.85, £46.93
2: A, B, C, D, E
3: 36m, 56m, 48m, 72m, 60m
4: £5.45, £5.30, £4.95, £5.95, £5.25
5: A, B, C, D, E
6: 18, 19, 17, 21, 15

© IPS Educational Publishing 2011

Multiple choice answer sheet.   Tests 13 to 18.

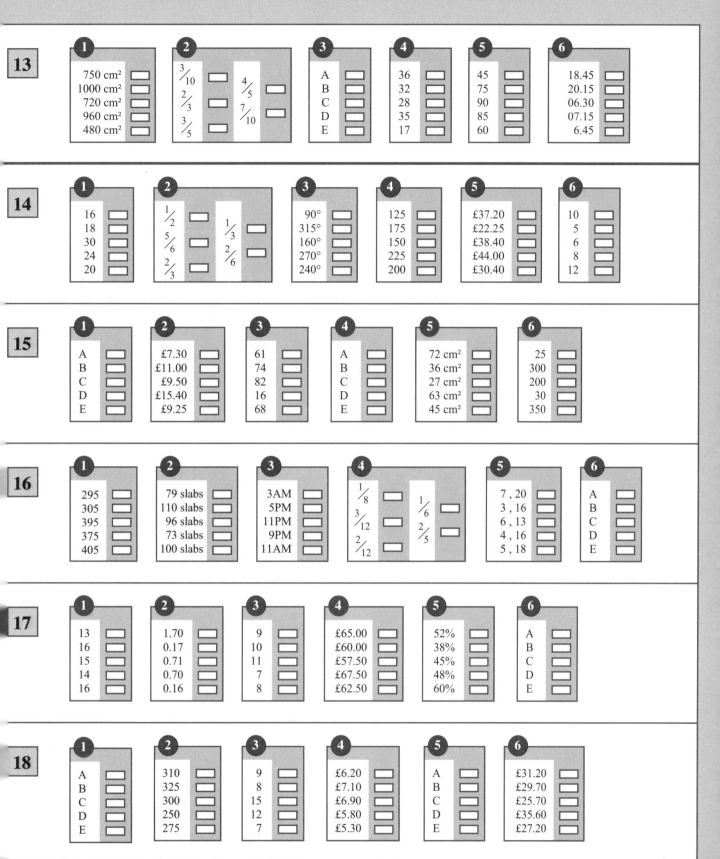

13

1
750 cm² ☐
1000 cm² ☐
720 cm² ☐
960 cm² ☐
480 cm² ☐

2
3/10 ☐   4/5 ☐
2/3 ☐
3/5 ☐   7/10 ☐

3
A ☐
B ☐
C ☐
D ☐
E ☐

4
36 ☐
32 ☐
28 ☐
35 ☐
17 ☐

5
45 ☐
75 ☐
90 ☐
85 ☐
60 ☐

6
18.45 ☐
20.15 ☐
06.30 ☐
07.15 ☐
6.45 ☐

14

1
16 ☐
18 ☐
30 ☐
24 ☐
20 ☐

2
1/2 ☐   1/3 ☐
5/6 ☐   2/6 ☐
2/3 ☐

3
90° ☐
315° ☐
160° ☐
270° ☐
240° ☐

4
125 ☐
175 ☐
150 ☐
225 ☐
200 ☐

5
£37.20 ☐
£22.25 ☐
£38.40 ☐
£44.00 ☐
£30.40 ☐

6
10 ☐
5 ☐
6 ☐
8 ☐
12 ☐

15

1
A ☐
B ☐
C ☐
D ☐
E ☐

2
£7.30 ☐
£11.00 ☐
£9.50 ☐
£15.40 ☐
£9.25 ☐

3
61 ☐
74 ☐
82 ☐
16 ☐
68 ☐

4
A ☐
B ☐
C ☐
D ☐
E ☐

5
72 cm² ☐
36 cm² ☐
27 cm² ☐
63 cm² ☐
45 cm² ☐

6
25 ☐
300 ☐
200 ☐
30 ☐
350 ☐

16

1
295 ☐
305 ☐
395 ☐
375 ☐
405 ☐

2
79 slabs ☐
110 slabs ☐
96 slabs ☐
73 slabs ☐
100 slabs ☐

3
3AM ☐
5PM ☐
11PM ☐
9PM ☐
11AM ☐

4
1/8 ☐   1/6 ☐
3/12 ☐   2/5 ☐
2/12 ☐

5
7 , 20 ☐
3 , 16 ☐
6 , 13 ☐
4 , 16 ☐
5 , 18 ☐

6
A ☐
B ☐
C ☐
D ☐
E ☐

17

1
13 ☐
16 ☐
15 ☐
14 ☐
16 ☐

2
1.70 ☐
0.17 ☐
0.71 ☐
0.70 ☐
0.16 ☐

3
9 ☐
10 ☐
11 ☐
7 ☐
8 ☐

4
£65.00 ☐
£60.00 ☐
£57.50 ☐
£67.50 ☐
£62.50 ☐

5
52% ☐
38% ☐
45% ☐
48% ☐
60% ☐

6
A ☐
B ☐
C ☐
D ☐
E ☐

18

1
A ☐
B ☐
C ☐
D ☐
E ☐

2
310 ☐
325 ☐
300 ☐
250 ☐
275 ☐

3
9 ☐
8 ☐
15 ☐
12 ☐
7 ☐

4
£6.20 ☐
£7.10 ☐
£6.90 ☐
£5.80 ☐
£5.30 ☐

5
A ☐
B ☐
C ☐
D ☐
E ☐

6
£31.20 ☐
£29.70 ☐
£25.70 ☐
£35.60 ☐
£27.20 ☐

© IPS Educational Publishing 2011

Multiple choice answer sheet.   Tests 19 & 20.

19

1
15 ☐
8 ☐
13 ☐
16 ☐
17 ☐

2
A ☐
B ☐
C ☐
D ☐
E ☐

3
16 Kg ☐
20 Kg ☐
22 Kg ☐
18 Kg ☐
24 Kg ☐

4
A ☐
B ☐
C ☐
D ☐
E ☐

5
£23.50 ☐
£28.50 ☐
£18.00 ☐
£29.00 ☐
£20.50 ☐

6
A ☐
B ☐
C ☐
D ☐
E ☐

20

1
2 , 9 ☐
2 , 4 ☐
9 , 2 ☐
9 , 4 ☐
4 , 9 ☐

2
A ☐
B ☐
C ☐
D ☐
E ☐

3
48 cm² ☐
80 cm² ☐
72 cm² ☐
64 cm² ☐
33 cm² ☐

4
A ☐
B ☐
C ☐
D ☐
E ☐

5
19.94 ☐
19.948 ☐
19.95 ☐
19.940 ☐
19.90 ☐

6
24 ☐
54 ☐
57 ☐
60 ☐
58 ☐

© IPS Educational Publishing 2011

Answers

	Test 1	Test 2	Test 3	Test 4	Test 5
1	A and D	350 grams	120	£4.15	C
2	£33.00	$\frac{2}{3}$	36	A	12
3	59	60°	13.45	34	8
4	E	150	2500cm³	£40.00	89
5	75cm²	£38.50	$\frac{3}{8}$	£40	D 6,2 A 2,6
6	15 boxes	18	16	12.10PM	43 packets

	Test 6	Test 7	Test 8	Test 9	Test 10
1	12, 9	14	£5.61	£11.55	$\frac{5}{8}$
2	B	C	B and E	42%	15 and 4
3	126 cm²	£14.00	£102.00	E	D
4	B	D	A	14	452 DVDs
5	90.985	C	£80.00	6.8	82 m
6	127	45 Kg	g = 14	24	1.30PM

	Test 11	Test 12	Test 13	Test 14	Test 15
1	41	£46.93	1000 cm²	16	A and D
2	Y 4,5 X 8,7	B	$\frac{7}{10}$	$\frac{1}{3}$	£11.00
3	13	72 metres	A	270°	74
4	E	£5.45	36	175	D
5	9	D	90	£44.00	45 cm²
6	24	17 boxes	18.45	6	300

	Test 16	Test 17	Test 18	Test 19	Test 20
1	395	13	B	17	9, 2
2	79 slabs	0.17	250	E	C
3	9.00PM	7	t = 12	22 Kg	64 cm²
4	$\frac{1}{6}$	£67.50	£5.30	A and E	D
5	3 and 16	48%	E	£29.00	19.95
6	C	C	£31.20	D	54

© IPS Educational Publishing 2011